Doe Eyed Venus

Elmast Kozloyan

SADIE GIRL PRESS

© 2014 Inside the Lantern Press
in collaboration with
Sadie Girl Press
2nd Printing 2016

Suggested reading based on cover art

If you see a pair of fairies or winged creatures

Turn to page(s) 3, 6, 7, and 8

If you see two figures in love or in conflict

Turn to page(s) 1, 2, 6, 7, 13, 14 and 15

If you see a raging bull or devilish horns

Turn to page(s) 9, 10, 11, 14, and 17

If you see an animal (e.g. a wolf, fox, rabbit or giraffe)

Turn to page(s) 3, 8, and 14

If you see body parts (e.g. legs or a pelvis)

Turn to page(s) 1, 4, 5, 6, and 15

Table of Contents

Table of Contents

I saw a busboy that looked just like you

My heart jumped
when we locked eyes
he put dinner rolls on my table
I found myself fantasizing about him
me and the dish of butter
melting next to
warm buns

Avocado Sunrise

The day I skipped a philosophy lecture
on logic and *modus ponens* arguments
was the day avocados became an erotic fruit

You greeted me at the door
fresh out of the shower
The smell of spicy cologne and recreational drugs
permeated my nose as I was pulled inside for a kiss
Our stomachs growled almost in unison
You suggested eggs
Although I was hungry for something else
         eggs will do for now
I'd never seen a man pick up a skillet
outside of television
Pleasantly surprised if not slightly aroused
         crack
                  sizzle
                           serve
Topped with avocadoes from your tree

If I like avocados, then I will make your sun rise
I like avocados

Licked a green shmear off your stubbled cheek
Took one last bite
and watched the rising sun peak through the avocado tree

Honey Water

Golden monarch wings
molded over her breasts
Scarlet poppy stems
wound around her tongue
The new moon's curve
mirrored in her thighs
of glowing ivory
anointed with lilac hued oil
Ethereal invocations
spilled from her lips
like honey water

North View*

Lavish gifts had been laid out
all for her
He had not arrived just yet
She ran her fingertips across
opalescent silk lingerie
that glowed on satin sheets
She slipped into the sheer fabric
Nestled herself into soft pale green cushions
Parted her lips and smiled
as she inhaled sweet perfumes
let out a satisfied moan
curled her toes
Her breasts bobbed
like water balloons
about to pop

*from Lisa Yuskavage's painting *North View*

Waiting in the bathtub

Lilac perfumes
Cinnamon sweet oils
Orange blossom candles
melting by our bedside
Champagne chilling in the fridge
next to a bowl of cherries
and chocolate sauce
Glasses are by the stove
little strawberries in each

Hybrid Rapture

I've taken centaurs for a ride
brushed their mane
fed them sugar cubes
Fawns are too
feminine for me
Mermen are manageable
until oxygen tanks run low
their slippery scales make them difficult
to hang onto
Elves are nice to have around
repairing my shoes
baking me cookies
Giants tend to leave you
in their stride
Satyrs can go on all night
leaving you exhausted
and picking off fur the next day

Yet there is something about
a frame mirroring my own
four limbs
fairly hairless
lacking hooves
wing
horns

Sweet Tea Mysteries

She slept in a bed filled with goat men
Limbs tangled into an anthropomorphic blob
Their soft tuffs of fur and faint bleating lulled her to sleep
only to be tossed out with one swift kick
She had grown accustomed to the bruises and shedding
Dryads living in the box plants
spun ivory webs around her bare skin
The sirens insisted they bathe her
she opted for a centaur rosewood oil massage
Outside the giants were harvesting
bleeding pomegranates
honeysuckle nectar
sacred lotus root
She walked past it all until she reached the car
Hermes had glued gold feathers onto her shoes
Her change of clothes were covered in opalescent dust
Cleaned them off and drove away

He waited for her in the coffee shop
Chatted over poppy seed bagels and sweet tea
He never questioned the glitter on her face
dark curls of hair in her sweater
or why she never took him home
He would never believe
          no matter how much she wished he could

Children of the Moon

Iridescent glass orbs
hum as they strike one another
Celestial hymns vibrate above
Blessed moon babies coo below
Pure
Untouched
Feather cradles
drifting about
Swaddled in strawberry pink
tuffs of dark curls beneath your cap
Swaying towards me
I knew you were mine

Injected

One hand scraped away at the faded ducky sticker
that sat atop canary yellow walls
The other was thrust forward
An offering
     an obedient offering
They looked down at my arm
annoyed
frustrated
at my small undistinguished veins
They missed the first few attempts
     I think the following five were on purpose
Eventually They hit scarlet
infused Their snake oil
and commenced the cotton clotting

The ducky was successfully removed

The Noose or the Knife

Creatures of her own design
menace
observe
at the edge of her sanity

She begs them to take her
       They refuse
Take it all!
       Leave her to rot

A remedy
Hidden within glass bottles
cushioned with cotton balls
Chalk stained tongues

Silver scalpel carving
frontal lobes
chopped like carrots
served with peas

Restraint to the point of hysteria
mind infected
poisoned voices
Cut and left out to dry

Pearl

I didn't come
for your pearls
      but I'll take them anyway
You place a diamond
on my tongue
I swallow
spit out steel nails
to your feet

Glide gems
over my body
until my skin
absorbs their pigmentation
Glowing
aurora-esque hues

In a certain light
your eyes
glare gold
and pupils elongate
Your tongue
flickers as you speak
Thumbing cigarette
ash on my forehead
Tequila tranquil-
izers shot up my throat

11

Removal

Can I rip off your tattoos?
like little stickers
Lick clean any remnants
of the adhesive
or blood
should I pull too forcefully

Letters to a Nymphette

Νύμφη – a marriageable young woman
Nymph – a mythological spirit of nature imagined as a
beautiful maiden inhabiting rivers, woods, or other
locations
Nymphomaniac – a woman who has abnormally excessive
and uncontrollable sexual desire

Child bearing hips
that sway and seduce
A solar eclipse that could blind
an unsuspecting fool who stares too long
Curious minds coveting a closer look
Yearning lips craving flesh
What they took, could never be returned
thrust thrum hum
Innocence lost with one swift hand
left lost to collect the shards
she would never understand why
kneel swallow wallow

From the girl once fit to wed
and the *slut* only taken to bed

Weaving Webs

Spindle silk strands
An imbued gift
woven to perfection
Invisible
to a certain slant of light
Erotic tales
laced in spiral threading
                    Wait

He won't notice at first
until he's tangled in your hard work
Knit knots
Nibble for taste
and seasoning
Bat your eight eyes
wink four
Say that you love him
Devour him whole

                    Repeat

Right of Passage

I wanted to kill him
so I did
It seemed like the rite thing to do
I stretched his limbs
Tied them down
 to point
    North
West   East
    South
I burned his right arm
Froze his left leg
then amputated
just shy of living flesh
Continued this pattern
until he could take no more
sage burned
blood shed
sob-blinded
It was better he did not see
I carved out his heart
snipped a lock of hair
and placed them in a silver case
Disposed of the remains
and went to bed

I don't have time for boys anyway

Acknowledgments

Thank you to the publications in which these poems first appeared:
"I saw a busboy that looked just like you" and "North View" in *Poetry in Motion*
"Honey Water", "Pearl", and "Letters to a Nymphette" in *East Jasmine Review*
"Children of the Moon" in *Milestone*
"The Noose or the Knife" in *Neat Magazine*
"Sweet Tea Mysteries" in *pacificREVIEW*
"Removal" in *Cadence Collective*
"Right of Passage" in *San Gabriel Valley Poetry Quarterly*

Special Thanks
To my family and friends for your ongoing support and love, a simple thank you will never be enough to express my gratitude.

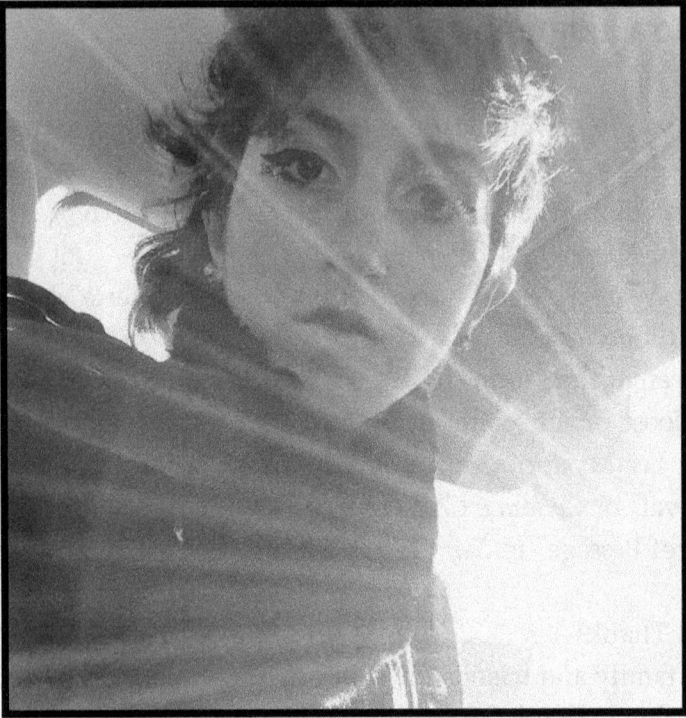

About the Author

Elmast Kozloyan is a poet trapped in limbo between magic and reality (though seldom chooses the latter). At the age of fifteen won silver for poetry in the Scholastic Art and Writing Awards and since then has been mentoring youth poets and published in places such as *Cadence Collective*, *Neat Magazine*, *Poetry in Motion*, *Pacific Review*, and the *East Jasmine Review*.